PETS' GUIDES

Goldie's Guide to

Caring for Your Goldfish

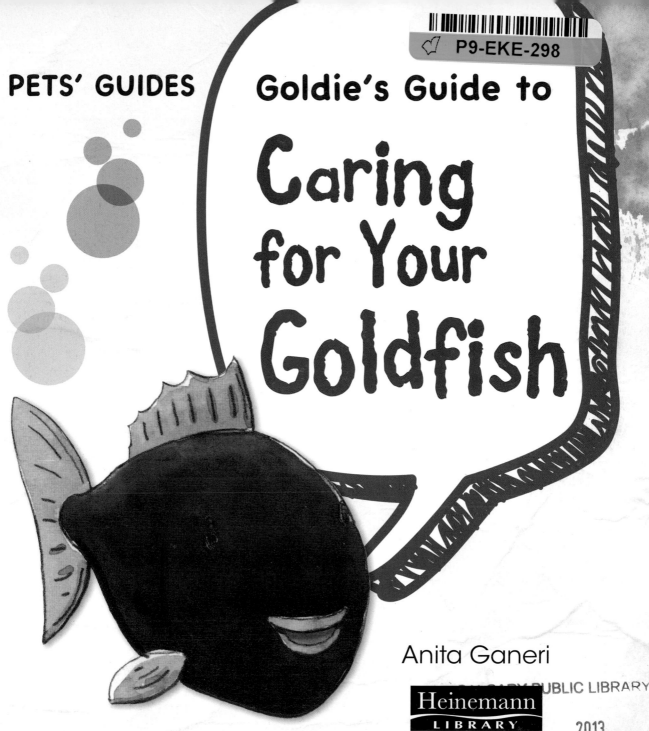

Anita Ganeri

Heinemann
LIBRARY
Chicago, Illinois

Edited by Daniel Nunn, Rebecca Rissman, and Sian Smith
Designed by Cynthia Della-Rovere
Original illustrations © Capstone Global Library Ltd 2013
Illustrated by Rick Peterson
Picture research by Tracy Cummins
Production by Victoria Fitzgerald
Originated by Capstone Global Library Ltd
Printed in China

17 16 15 14 13 12
10 9 8 7 6 5 4 3 2 1

Library of Congress Cataloging-in-Publication Data
Ganeri, Anita, 1961-
Goldie's guide to caring for your goldfish / Anita Ganeri.—1st ed.
        p. cm.—(Pets' guides)
Includes bibliographical references and index.

ISBN 978-1-4329-7132-8 (hb)—ISBN 978-1-4329-7139-7 (pb) 1. Goldfish—Juvenile literature. I. Title.
SF458.G6G366 2013
639.3'7484—dc23   2012017280

Acknowledgments
The author and publisher are grateful to the following for permission to reproduce copyright material: Alamy pp. 21 (© Juniors Bildarchiv), 23 (© Pink Sun Media), 25 (© fishpix); Capstone Library pp. 7, 11, 13, 17, 19, 27 (Karon Dubke); Corbis p. 5 (© Michael Pole); Getty Images p. 9 (Justin Sullivan); iStockphoto p. 15 (© polarica).

Cover photograph of a goldfish reproduced with permission of Superstock (© age fotostock).

We would like to thank Ray Rich, from the Goldfish Society of Great Britain, for his invaluable help in the preparation of this book.

Every effort has been made to contact copyright holders of any material reproduced in this book. Any omissions will be rectified in subsequent printings if notice is given to the publisher.

All the Internet addresses (URLs) given in this book were valid at the time of going to press. However, due to the dynamic nature of the Internet, some addresses may have changed, or sites may have changed or ceased to exist since publication. While the author and publisher regret any inconvenience this may cause readers, no responsibility for any such changes can be accepted by either the author or the publisher.

Contents

Some words are shown in bold, **like this**. You can find out what they mean by looking in the glossary.

Do You Want a Pet Goldfish?

Hi! I'm Goldie the goldfish, and I'm very pleased to meet you. If you're thinking of getting a goldfish as a pet, you have come to the right place. This book is all about fish like me and what great pets we make!

Goldfish like me need to be looked after properly for our whole lives. You will need to feed me every day and find me a clean, safe place to live with plenty of space. Otherwise, I can easily become unhappy and sick.

Choosing Your Fish

Fish come in lots of different sizes and colors. Common goldfish like me can be golden-red or have patches of yellow, silver, black, or white. Some types of goldfish have long, trailing fins and tails.

You can buy your goldfish from a pet shop, a garden center, or a fish **breeder**. Goldfish like living together so you can keep a few of us, as long as your tank is big enough.

Healthy Goldfish

Make sure that you pick a healthy goldfish. Watch me swimming around in my tank. If I'm lively and active and my fins are strong and upright, I'm probably a good choice. A fish that has split or damaged fins or is very thin may not be well.

Your new goldfish should also have shiny skin and bright, clear eyes. Before buying your fish, look around the shop. If the shop is clean and well looked after, it is more likely that the fish will be healthy, too.

Getting Ready

Before you bring me home for the first time, you need to get a few things ready. The most important thing to have is a large tank with plenty of room for me to swim around in. Here is the rest of my goldfish homecoming shopping list…

Goldie's Shopping List

- tap water
- **dechlorinator**
- a **water filter**
- gravel for the bottom of the tank
- **air pump** and **airline**
- water plants
- a small net for moving your goldfish
- a bucket
- goldfish food

Filling a Tank

You need to get my tank ready before you bring me home. Two days before I come home, fill my tank with tap water, mixed with **dechlorinator**. Then let the water warm up to **room temperature**. Attach the **water filter** to my tank and keep it turned on all the time. It will keep the water clean and healthy for me.

If my tank has only water in it, I'll soon get bored with living there. Put some gravel on the bottom to make it more interesting. Place my tank somewhere away from **drafts** and bright sunlight.

Breathing

Like all animals, I have to breathe a gas called **oxygen** to stay alive. I get oxygen from the water in my tank. To keep the amount of oxygen at just the right level, you need to attach an **air pump** to the tank.

Please also put some water plants in my tank. They make oxygen for me to breathe. I also like to swim around and hide among the leaves. Plant them firmly in the gravel on the bottom of the tank. They look best in groups of tall and short plants.

Welcome Home

The day has come for me to move into my new home. The pet shop will give you a large plastic bag filled with water to carry me in. Don't tip me straight into the tank. Otherwise, the shock of the different water temperature could make me sick.

Float the bag in the tank for 20 minutes. Leaving the bag in the water makes sure that the water temperature is the same in the bag as it is in the tank. Then catch me in a net and put me into my new home.

Feeding Time

It's time for my breakfast! Feed me special goldfish flakes or **pellets** that you can buy from a pet shop. Sprinkle them on the water. Then watch me swim to the surface to munch up my food.

Please feed me twice a day, in the morning and evening. Be careful not to give me too much food. If there is any food left after 15 minutes, scoop it out with a net. Otherwise, it may go bad and make me sick.

Cleaning the Tank

Goldfish like me like a nice, clean tank. Pieces of old food, dead leaves, and fish poo can make the water dirty. Check the water every day to make sure that it is clean. I can quickly become sick in a dirty tank.

Every week or two, change half of the water in the tank. Make sure the water you put back is at **room temperature**. Clean the tank thoroughly. Use a scraper to clean any green slime off the inside of the glass.

Fish in Ponds

Like all goldfish, I'll grow up and get bigger, so please make sure that my tank is big enough for me and my friends. Goldfish don't like an **overcrowded** tank, so you might have to buy a new, bigger one for us.

wire mesh

If I grow longer than about five inches, I can't live in a tank anymore. I need to go and live in an outside pond. You might have one in your backyard. Cover the pond with wire mesh to stop birds and cats from trying to catch me.

Sick Goldfish

If you look after me properly, I should stay healthy for many years. If I start swimming slowly, my fins droop, or I stop eating my food, I may be sick, so call the vet. The vet will be able to find out what is wrong with me.

white lump

Look out for white lumps on my body and fins. These are also signs that I may have a nasty illness. The vet will give you some medicine for me, but you may need to move me to my own tank until I'm better.

Going Away

If you're going on vacation, please make sure that someone else takes care of me. They should feed me every other day with a small amount of food, and change one-third of the water in my tank about every five days.

Leave your friends a supply of food and everything they need to look after me. Write a note of how much food they should give me. It can make me sick if I eat too much. You should also leave them a telephone number for the vet.

Goldfish Facts

- Goldfish were first kept as pets in China more than a thousand years ago. They belong to the carp family.

- The biggest pet goldfish on record measured 19 inches long.

- A goldfish usually lives for about 5 to 10 years, but the oldest goldfish known is an amazing 49 years old.

- People used to think that goldfish could only remember things for a few seconds. In fact, their memories last for 3 to 5 months.

- Goldfish can learn to recognize different human faces and voices.

Helpful Tips

- Feed your goldfish regularly, but do not feed it too much. Your goldfish should always seem to be hungry and should never ignore the food you give it.

- Never keep your goldfish in a goldfish bowl. There would not be enough **oxygen** for your goldfish to breathe and it may die.

- Types of water plants you can put in your tank are:

    elodea—these root in the gravel

    hornwort—these float in the top part of the tank

    duckweed—these float on the surface

- Make sure that your tank is kept covered and out of reach of cats and other pets.

Glossary

airline a tube that carries air from the air pump into your tank

air pump a machine attached to your tank that puts oxygen in the water for your fish to breathe

breeder someone who keeps goldfish for sale

dechlorinator chemicals you add to the water in your fish tank to make it safe

drafts blasts of cold air that come through windows or under doors

overcrowded when too many things are put into a small space

oxygen a gas that animals need to breathe to stay alive

pellets small lumps of food

room temperature the usual temperature of a room in your home

water filter a machine attached to your tank that keeps the water clean

Find Out More

Books

Slade, Suzanne. *Fish: Finned and Gilled Animals.*
Mankato, Minn.: Capstone, 2010.

Tourville, Amanda Doering. *Flutter and Float: Bringing
Home Goldfish.* Mankato, Minn.: Capstone, 2009.

Internet Sites

Facthound offers a safe, fun way to
find Internet sites related to this book.
All of the sites on Facthound have been
researched by our staff.

Here's all you do: Visit www.facthound.com
Type in this code: 9781432971328

Index